How to
Pray Always

Also by Raoul Plus
from Sophia Institute Press®:

Winning Souls for Christ

Raoul Plus

How to Pray Always

SOPHIA INSTITUTE PRESS®
Manchester, New Hampshire

How to Pray Always was originally published in 1926 by Burns, Oates, and Washbourne, Ltd., London, England. This 2003 edition by Sophia Institute Press® contains minor editorial revisions to the original text.

Printed in the United States of America

Sophia Institute Press®
Box 5284, Manchester, NH 03108
1-800-888-9344
www.sophiainstitute.com

Nihil obstat: Edward Mahoney, S.T.D., *Censor deputatus*
Imprimatur: Edmund Can. Surmont, *Vicarius generalis*
Westminster, March 29, 1926

Library of Congress Cataloging-in-Publication Data

Sheen, Fulton J. (Fulton John), 1895-1979.
Victory over vice / Fulton J. Sheen.
p. cm.
ISBN 1-928832-30-X (pbk. : alk. paper)
1. Jesus Christ — Seven last words — Meditations.
2. Deadly sins — Meditations. I. Title.
BT457 .S54 2004
232.96'35 — dc22 2003024655

Contents

Editor's note: The biblical quotations in the following pages are taken from the Douay-Rheims edition of the Old and New Testaments. Where applicable, quotations have been cross-referenced with the differing names and enumeration in the Revised Standard Version, using the following symbol: (RSV =).

Introduction

Our Lord taught us to "pray without ceasing."[1] Now, how far is it possible to put this ideal into practice, and how much is really attainable? How can the implications of this injunction be reconciled with the requirements of our psychological self and our daily life? How can we reach a right understanding of the conflicting call of the invisible world within us and the imperious and quite legitimate demands of the visible world outside us, and reconcile the attractions of a life that we would like to be as contemplative as possible with the duties of an active life?

In a few words, how is it possible to reach a correct understanding of the meaning of recollection and the correct balance between generosity and wisdom?

It is these points that will be explained in these pages.

Three basic principles govern our considerations:

[1] Thess. 5:17.

- A *principle of psychology:* it is impossible (exceptional cases apart) to fix our minds always upon God.
- A *moral principle:* to be one with God in will is better than continual recollection.
- A *principle of ascetic theology:* the frequent thought of God is of great assistance in reaching the intimate union of our will with God's.

These ideas may be expressed more briefly without interfering with subsequent fuller explanations, by saying:

- To think always of God is impossible.
- To think always of God is not necessary.
- It is most profitable to think often of God.

These three principles having been laid down, it remains to be seen how the practice of a life of perfect recollection is governed by three laws: to pray well; to turn everything into prayer; and to develop a spirit of prayer.

How to Pray Always

Part One

The Principles of Prayer

Chapter One

Learn to be recollected

There is a distinction to be made at the outset that will throw a strong light upon the problem of thinking always of God. We must be on our guard to avoid confusing the *act* of prayer with the *state* of prayer. Further on we shall see in what consists the state of prayer.

An act of prayer may be either vocal or mental, according as it is formed of words recited by the lips, or is the inner cry of the soul expressed in formulated or unformulated transports of love, or in the silence of union with God. In these two cases, our thoughts are occupied or trying to be occupied with God.

Our acts of prayer are the moments when our thoughts are in loving union with God. The problem is this: can these moments of loving union with our Lord be brought so close together that they form one almost continuous chain of thought? More briefly: can my thoughts be absorbed without intermission with God? Is it possible to think of nothing but Him?

No. Here lies a double impediment. First, the practical impossibility: our daily duties involve a number of actions other than formulated acts of prayer. There may be a lesson to prepare, a lecture to give, some household task or work of charity to be attended to, or an engrossing intellectual study to be undertaken. And if it is true that it is very difficult to think of one thing while doing another, in most cases and for most people, an occupation, even when only external, absorbs all their energies, including those of the mind. This is due to our natural frailty.

Later we shall endeavor to show how a wise method can somewhat get over this obstacle, but the fact remains. Hemmed in as we are by the visible world of sense, it is only with difficulty that we can have even fragmentary relations with the invisible world. Man is created with a body and soul, and no one can ask of others or require of himself to lead a life of pure spirit.

To this practical difficulty is added another of a psychological character. Even if our occupations were reduced to the minimum, and if, as is the case with a contemplative vocation, we were able to spend a large portion of time in prayer, continuous prayers would still be impossible, for they would soon lead to grave mental derangement and complete powerlessness.

Learn to be recollected

We are not archangels. Even the timetable of the contemplative orders is interspersed with occupations other than contemplative prayer. No one can be continually adding fresh prayers to his usual exercises. It is an illusion, then, to wish never to lose the recollection of God for one instant. Our mental powers are incapable of this.

Doubtless God can endow the soul with special faculties, so as to enable it to live always or nearly always with the thought or consciousness of His presence. In such a case, the ability to remain in the presence of God is not the normal result of our own efforts. It is the action of God, who delights in overwhelming the soul. He enfolds it in a recollection that is more or less impenetrable to outside disturbances. Mystical writers call this *infused recollection*, to distinguish it from that which is the result of our own efforts and is called *acquired recollection*. This recollection can progress from the simple mystical touch, which is temporary and often of very short duration, to a union that is continuous. In this case, recollection is permanent, suffering no eclipse of the beloved presence and its enjoyment.

At first, this may lead to moments of such entire absorption that the soul is more or less unfitted to take its place in its accustomed surroundings; that which is seen within is so different from the painted canvas of the outside world. But in the highest stage of union, the soul finds it can easily adjust its sense life to harmonize with its supernatural life; outwardly it behaves like everyone else, while keeping within perpetual contact with the Divine Master. It is bound and it is free, and all the freer for being bound to Him who is sovereign liberty, on whom it is entirely dependent.

The masters of the spiritual life are unanimous in recognizing that persons who are favored with this highest degree of union with God are rare. They are less in agreement over the question as to whether there are few or many who are endowed with periods of infused recollection. They are unanimous in reckoning that, in all probability, this infused power of recollection is unattainable by human means, and that none can claim it as a right, however great their efforts may have been. It is the opinion of some writers that if someone who is mentally adaptable and subject to no hindrances gives himself up to leading a prayerful and mortified life in as perfect a degree as possible, he will in fact reach the state of infused recollection, although it is in no sense his due. They declare that God is so desirous of giving Himself that whenever He finds one who is well disposed and detached, He will most certainly communicate Himself. Others question this statement. It is true that man was created for the vision of God, but that will be granted to him at the end of his earthly existence.

We walk by faith as wayfarers in this world. To say that every mortified soul is called upon to quit this life of faith and enter now into direct possession is to turn these persons into merely semiwayfarers. Another objection is that there are persons who have practiced detachment during the course of a long life, yet in spite of apparently being quite suitable, they have never experienced even the shadow of a mystical favor.

This is not the place to take part in a discussion of this sort. In every case, infused recollection, whether it be the outcome of acquired recollection or not, is in itself and by right independent of our own efforts, so that it is impossible to lay down technical rules concerning it, and still less to give any infallible advice as to how to prepare for it.

It is difficult to think continuously of God for any length of time

Acquired recollection is quite another thing. It depends entirely upon ourselves, aided, of course, by the grace of God, but grace of a usual character.

All the same, it is necessary to define the extent and limitations of the power of man over his imagination, senses, and thoughts. Man has direct control over his thoughts. We can think about what we like. But our authority over the imagination and senses is different. Here we have only indirect control. Mental pictures and reactions find their way in and work away within us without our assistance; indeed, often they are against us.

All we can do is place ourselves in a favorable environment amid peaceful conditions. But I cannot prevent that idea from crossing my brain. I may try to forbid the entrance of certain ideas into my mind, yet they will come in all the same, but at any rate I shall not have given them any assistance.

The imagination and feeling are a couple of giddypates. I may circumscribe their field of action, but to keep them entirely within bounds is impossible. At the very moment I am most anxious to be at peace, when saying my prayers or during some engrossing work, they worm their way in and sometimes take complete possession of my thoughts.

The conclusion to be drawn from these psychological truths is that the possibility of success in recollection is both very great and very small.

The possibility is small because our memory and imagination are incessantly trying to distract our attention in spite of us, and sometimes God only knows how they manage to do it. St. Jerome in the desert was tormented by the thought of Roman festivities; St. Antony by fantastic visions, which are depicted for us in sacred art.[2]

The possibility is great, for do we not have the power at each moment of forcibly recalling some incident or idea to our mind, and above all, are we not our own masters, and able to drive away the proximate causes of distraction?

Every spiritual writer insists upon this point when speaking of the remote preparation for prayer.

If we madly throw ourselves into worldly, frivolous amusements and pleasures, even though they are quite harmless, we have no right to complain of remaining for long moments without thinking of God, and of spiritual dryness and dullness at prayer.

"I really tried to pray," we say, "and I can do nothing. It is quite sufficient for me to kneel down for distractions to come tumbling into my mind immediately, like sparrows

[2] St. Jerome (c. 342-420), Doctor who translated the Bible into Latin; St. Antony (251-356), desert monk and father of Western monasticism.

fluttering down to pick up crumbs, and for them to torment me without a second's respite."

But what about the crumbs you collected when you left your mind open to every form of distraction, idle conversations, frivolous books, and inquisitiveness? Naturally, once you were still, your imagination had full play with all these thoughts.

There is an art in keeping a watch over our thoughts, in clearing the brain, in sifting our impressions, and in getting rid of idle fancies. If every trivial thought can enter the mind as if it were a mill, and cast any rubbish it likes under the grindstone, whose fault is it that later on, instead of the homogeneous white flour of pure wheat, there is only worthless chaff?

As nothing can be really destroyed unless something else takes its place, so the difficulty is less how to drive away useless impressions and ideas from the mind and the imagination, than to suggest some profitable thoughts to these two faculties; we should try to live habitually with a number of holy impressions and ideas stored up in our minds.

Hence, we discover a curiously vicious circle. The best means of preserving habitual recollection is fidelity to prayer. The best condition for praying well is habitual recollection.

It is not without reason that St. Ignatius[3] recommends that the man who wishes to pray well prepare the subject of his prayer on the preceding evening, so as to occupy his memory. Then he goes to rest with these thoughts in his mind; on waking, he will call to mind the subject matter of his meditation, prepared the evening before, and think quietly about it while dressing. This is the advice of one who was a master of asceticism and also an expert in psychology.

When the moment for prayer arrives, he recommends that if the person is alone, he shall not immediately kneel down, but remain standing some distance away and reflect upon the presence of God there in that room, then kiss the ground as an act of humiliation and so associate the body with the religious attitude of the mind.

This is the immediate preparation, which complete the remote preparation. It is easy to call these mere details; anyone who has really tried to meditate will readily allow that this is sensible advice. The Church has the same end in view when she tells us on entering church to take holy water and make the Sign of the Cross. Her aim is

[3] St. Ignatius of Loyola (1491-1556), founder of the Society of Jesus.

to impress upon the mind of the incomer the idea of the proximity of God. It is a great mistake to try to pray as some people do, immediately after leaving some absorbing work, without any interval, and then, as soon as they are on their knees, expect their mind to be at rest and divine thoughts to come flowing in.

Man is one complete whole; there are no water-tight compartments in him. Our whole self enters into every movement of our activity. It requires extraordinary agility of mind to be able to leave behind on the other side of the door everything that would be a hindrance to our devotions. Sometimes, in spite of our good intentions and determined efforts, it is impossible to control our thoughts during prayer. How much more likely is this to occur if the will has not foreseen and guarded against the approach of danger?

The practicc of prayer, also, is the best preparation for a recollected life.

It is necessary to introduce into the mind a number of ideas and impressions that will be of use in prayer. Nothing will be of greater assistance than the fixed determination to come into close contact with God daily. To quote the words of the foundress of the Oblates of the Sacred Heart, Louise de Montaignac, "It is by accustoming ourselves to making acts of love at regular moments that we shall learn the good habit of being able to turn to God at all times."

It is a foolish mistake to expect to lead a recollected life that is not also a life of prayer. The best method of learning to pray always is to pray whenever it is possible, and as well as is possible.

Chapter Two

Submit your will to God's will

Father Quadrapani the Barnabite tells us in one of his books, "To do all our actions for God is worth more than thinking about Him."

This statement, if rightly understood, is quite correct. But it has nothing to do with deciding whether the active or the contemplative life is the more perfect state. This question was settled long ago, and is quite outside the present considerations. It matters not whether a life be contemplative or not, in the cloister or in the world.

The point is this: what is it that God asks of us, apart from the times of stated prayer? Is it to think about Him, or rather, and above all, to do our actions for Him? Is it our mind that He wants, or our heart, our memory or our will? Unquestionably, it is our will. With the exception of the time of prayer, when our acts for God consist in thinking of Him, God demands that on every occasion we should be working for Him, even, if necessary, by restraining the thought of Him when — and the supposition is not fanciful — it would be to the detriment of our work for Him. A concrete example will make this clear.

A mother of a family with young children finds herself overburdened with urgent household tasks. Yet the morning finds her going off to Mass and absorbed in long and maybe fervent prayers, when prudence demands that she should stay at home and see to the care of the house. Is she following the exact path that God has traced out for her, or that an enlightened piety would require?

Or let us suppose that the morning Mass is possible, but that the mother, on her return to her family, is so absorbed by her pious thoughts that she does nothing well. The moments of prayer increase, her aspirations accumulate, but so do the garments to be mended, and all sorts of things are forgotten and left undone. Who would not advise, in a case like this, fewer pious exercises and greater fidelity to home duties?

It is quite clear that whenever duty requires us to pray, all our efforts should be exerted in trying to think about God as fully as possible.

Apart from this, where does our duty lie? It demands that the act of the present moment shall be done for God as perfectly as possible, that in all that I do, I shall not look for self-satisfaction, but that God alone shall be my final objective. This last sentence expresses in brief the whole theory of how to pray always.

To be always praying does not imply a succession of religious exercises one after the other — five decades of the Rosary followed by a little office, then a spiritual reading, with mental prayer to come after it, and so on — but to live in a state in which everything is the means whereby "the soul is lifted up to God." No one can attempt to turn his life into an uninterrupted succession of pious exercises, or the mental balance will be rapidly upset.

Our aim should be to guard against the danger of worldliness by acting always with a pure intention, so that our whole life may be offered up to God.

Continuous acts of prayer are impossible; the continuous *state* of prayer is highly desirable. The state of prayer consists in preserving a pure intention during the fulfillment of our daily tasks. I cannot have my thoughts occupied with God without interruption. But my will should never be directed toward any object except God, at any rate as its last end.

To refer all that we do implicitly, although not always explicitly, to God through this direct orientation of the will is a form of union with Him that is quite attainable and leads to perfection.

The difficulty then resolves itself into this: how to keep the will in this fixed direction toward God in all our actions. It is the whole problem of the direction of the intention. There are many ways of directing the intention toward God: by thinking of Him at the present moment (actual intention) or, without thinking of Him at this moment, by acting under the impulse of an intention formulated earlier, which still persists (virtual intention).

Some people are inclined to think that a habitual good intention is sufficient to render our acts supernaturally meritorious. They declare that because there has been no positive deviation from the path the soul has mapped out, it continues along the straight course toward God, and eternal merit is retained.

According to this hypothesis, every human act that is not bad tends toward God, and is therefore an act that can be supernaturalized and lifted up to God; it is at the same time a prayer and a meritorious act.

If we apply this statement to the virtual intention, all is well. In a fervent soul, the whole activity is governed by clearly defined supernatural motives, so that the virtual intention is nearly always present.

Therefore, in the life of a truly generous and Christlike soul, if we distinguish between prayers taken in the strict sense of the word and pious exercises on one hand, and, on the other, all its conscious activities, we find that everything is offered up to God, not only formal prayer, which is easily understood, but equally that which is not formal prayer, because it is also in accordance with the definition: "Prayer is the lifting up of the mind and soul to God."

Bossuet describes this secondary form of prayer: "It is the desire to praise God in all creatures and for all creatures by making the best use of them all, and sanctifying them by using them so that He may be glorified: the good use of light and darkness, of fine weather and rain, of fire and ice; the good use of all that exists and still more of myself, my eyes, my tongue, my mouth, my hands and feet, and my whole heart, and above all of my soul and my mind."[4]

In another place he says, "We must pray during the day, at night, and as often as we awake; and this continuous prayer does not consist in a perpetual tension of mind, but rather . . . [in] the keeping of ourselves in a state of dependence upon God as far as is possible, showing Him our needs — that is, silently laying them before Him. Thus, as the cracked, parched earth, by exposing her

[4] Jacques-Benigne Bossuet, *Letters*, Vol. 27.

parched surface to the sky, seems to be calling for rain, so the soul, by exposing her wants to God, appears to be saying, 'Lord, I have no need to pray to Thee; my needs, my state of indigence speak for me.' Thus, we pray without words, and God understands this language."[5]

A similar thought is expressed by a nun who writes: "I have always considered that, during the night, sleep is my best prayer. . . . Only, the whole of me is not sleeping, for my heart keeps watch by the tabernacle, and I ask my guardian angel to offer each heartbeat to our Lord as an act of love."[6]

St. Augustine[7] uses much the same idea in his explanation of the Thirty-Fourth Psalm to the Christians of Hippo: "If you are singing a hymn, you are praising God (always presupposing that you are thinking of the words). Then the hymn comes to an end, and it is time for a meal; if you keep yourself from overeating, you will be praising God. You go to your room to rest, and unless you get up with the set resolve to do something wrong, you will still

[5] Jacques-Benigne Bossuet, *Meditations on the Gospel*, Vol. 6.

[6] St. Agnes of the Cross.

[7] St. Augustine (354-430), Bishop of Hippo.

be praising God. You go off to your business, and so long as there are no fraudulent dealings, God will be praised. Are you a rural laborer? Then be sure that there are no weeds left in the ground you are digging, and once again, this will be an occasion of praising God. Thus, by the innocence of your works, you will be praising God all the day long."

To sum up: prayer is every act that is offered up to the Divine Majesty, to adore Him, give thanks to Him, and implore His grace; all is offered up to Him, whether it be explicit, formal prayer — that is, acts of prayer — or implicit, virtual prayer, which includes all our supernaturalized activities, the fulfillment of our daily duties from a supernatural intention.

This truth can be expressed in another way: we can pray by thought and by will: by thought when we perform our spiritual exercises, or by the offering of our whole being and its activities to God, which implies that all our ordinary duties are performed from a supernatural motive.

Our Lord is the model of the state of prayer

The state of prayer is devotion to our daily duties. The theory of this statement is clear, and the consequences are no less apparent. It would be a great mistake to imagine that, although our life has been supernaturalized, yet because we are not always thinking of God, therefore we cannot be living in union with Him. In the next chapter, we shall see how it is possible and even highly desirable that work for God and thoughts of God should be intermingled. But before all, it must clearly be understood that a supernatural life does not of necessity require the actual thought of God.

If this were the case, only those acts which are explicitly a matter for prayer are capable of being offered to God, which would reduce our supernatural activities to acts of piety. It is quite evident that we cannot sit apart in some corner, with hands clasped, thinking about God, nor is it asked of us.

Sometimes, as has been seen already, formal prayer has to give way to a more pressing daily duty. Our daily duties come first, before everything else. True union with God consists in the union of our will with the will of God. If, after many careful and well-weighed considerations, I can honestly say it is God's will that I should pray, then it is my duty to pray. But if I am obliged to leave my prayers in order to attend to my duties, even if those duties are of such an absorbing nature that my mind cannot find a moment's respite in which to turn my thoughts to God, my union with Him remains unbroken.

Sanctity is to be found in the union of our will with the will of God. What is it that our Lord says of Himself? "My meat" — that is, the substance, the mainspring of my life — "is to do the will of Him that sent me."[8] Mary, the most Christlike of all God's creatures, a Christian in the full sense of the word, answered the angel with the words: "Behold the handmaid of the Lord; be it done to me according to thy word."[9]

And we have nothing else to do but to act in all things in accordance with the divine will. We are not called to imitate our Lord in His birth in the manger with the beasts, or in His death on the Cross. We are asked to reproduce in our own lives His entire and radical submission in all things to the Father's will, which formed the foundation of His whole existence. The life of Christ consists essentially in this: He who is equal with His Father made Himself subordinate to Him, so that by His obedience, He could repair the first sin of disobedience. As the Word, He is equal with His Father; as man, He is inferior to Him.

[8] John 4:34.

[9] Luke 1:38.

The purpose of his earthly life becomes more defined: "He humbled Himself, becoming obedient unto death, even to the death of the Cross."[10] *Obedient unto death*. For thirty years of His life, He was subject. And the remainder of the time, He was still obedient. "For Christ did not please Himself";[11] He did not follow His own wishes in anything, for it would have meant that He was turning to His own use as man His activity which was centered in the Father. "Did you not know that I must be about my Father's business?"[12] He gave Himself up to do His Father's business even to the tragedy of Gethsemani and Calvary: "Not my will but Thine be done."[13] Up to the last moment of His earthly life, when ascending to His Father, He could say: "It is finished";[14] I have accomplished the task.

We ought to be returning perpetually to this fundamental idea. Each one of us, in order to realize the Christian ideal, should have the same center for his life as Christ in His human nature had for His, never taking our

[10] Phil. 2:8.

[11] Rom. 15:3.

[12] Luke 2:49.

[13] Luke 22:42.

[14] Cf. John 19:30.

individual wishes for the end and object of our being, but on all occasions choosing more or less formally and always effectively the "things of God," God's will.

Father Faber in a note in his book *Bethlehem*, quotes a saying of Mary of Agreda, who declares that our Lord revealed to her that He exercised the power of choice on only one occasion during His earthly life, and that was when He chose suffering.

If this is really "the Christ," every Christian, if he truly deserves to be called "another Christ," should make himself a replica, a copy of Him who was supremely obedient and submissive to the wishes and desires of the Father, so that in all things He saw only the Father's will. "He hath sent me,"[15] said Isaiah, in one of the most beautiful Messianic texts. Every Christian ought to reproduce in himself this ideal of the life of Christ.

To do this presupposes the death of our natural wishes, impulses, and desires. Self must be relegated to the background and not be permitted to interfere in the ordering of our lives, or it should be allowed to make itself heard only after God has spoken and always under His guidance. "I seek not my own will, but the will of Him that sent

[15] Isa. 61:1.

me."[16] "For I do always the things that please Him."[17] Thus, self is reduced to a subject condition by this inner obedience which is the perfect imitation of our Lord.

The same advice was given by St. Paul to those who desired to reproduce in themselves the life of Christ crucified. To be crucified with Christ is not to drive the nails into our hands and feet, but to bend ourselves to this absolute self-renunciation, which is like a living death.

To act for our own interests, by taking self as the ultimate aim, is to accomplish not an act that rises heavenward, but on the contrary, one that is decadent; it is to deflect some of our powers to self, this mean, petty self, taking self for the center, and is a departure from the perfect imitation of Christ, whereby we cease to be united with the will of God, and give up prayer.

It is almost superfluous to point out that this doctrine is simply the practical explanation of the foundations that St. Ignatius lays down in his book of *Spiritual Exercises*, and which is given in the catechism as the purpose of our existence: "to know, love, and serve God." Therefore, my life, my being, and my powers should have only God for

[16] John 5:30.

[17] John 8:29.

their last end. "In all that I have to do, there should be as little of self as possible"; at any rate not self as the productive cause — for I never do well that which I try to do by myself — nor self as my final objective. And this method of raising all my powers to God, without any intermixture of self, is nothing less than perfect prayer. It is the homage of all my life to Him who has an absolute right to the supreme homage of all that exists. We see how St. Ignatius in his book from the very first prepares the soul in the most solid manner for union with God.

The perfect prayer of the Church is the offering of the consecrated bread in the Mass. Now, in the Host in place of the bread there is our Lord Jesus Christ; the substance of the bread is there no longer. In the same way, my life will be a perfect prayer if there is no mingling of self-interest, if instead of self, there is Christ, and I am entirely submissive to the will of God.

Chapter Three

Practice interior silence

Let us see how far we have gotten. We cannot always be thinking of God, nor is it necessary. We can be constantly united with God without the constant thought of Him. The union of our will with the will of God is the sole form of union that is really requisite.

Wherein, then, lies the utility of the exercise of the presence of God enjoined by all the masters of the spiritual life? We will now explain.

As has been said, it is necessary to have an absolutely sure intention in all our actions, so that the generous fulfillment of our daily duties may be directed toward the highest supernatural ideal. Thus, our life, apart from moments of prayer, will be a prayerful life.

It is clear that the habit of giving an upward glance to God at the moment of action is a great assistance in aiding us to behave always with a pure intention and in freeing us from our natural impulses and fancies, so, that, retaining our self-mastery, or rather, God becoming the sole

Master, all our movements become dependent upon the Holy Spirit.

We see in the Gospel that whenever our Lord was about to undertake some important step, He always paused for a moment to raise His eyes to Heaven, and only after this moment of recollection did He take up the work He had to do. "He lifted up His eyes to Heaven"[18] is a phrase that recurs with significant frequency. And doubtless, when there was no outward sign of this prayer, there was the inward offering.

The ideal is the same for us. The constant subjection of self to the guidance of the Holy Spirit is made easier from the fact of His presence in the soul, where He is asked explicitly to preside over all our doings. It is impossible to put the spirit of recollection into generous practice unless there is also a deeply rooted spirit of self-renunciation. We shall not submit wholeheartedly to the invisible Guest unless He is kept in close proximity to us. The death of self cannot take place unless the spirit of life is already installed, unless it moves upon the face of the waters.[19]

[18] Cf. John 11:41; 17:1.

[19] Cf. Gen. 1:2.

Man will not consent to drive away the money-changers from the temple of his soul until he realizes that it is a Holy of Holies — not a house of traffic, but in very truth the house of God.

We thus reach two striking conclusions:

- There cannot be entire dependence upon the Holy Spirit's guidance, which is the true meaning of living in Christ, without complete self-renunciation.

- There cannot be complete self-renunciation without the constant underlying spirit of faith, without the habit of interior silence, a silence where God is dwelling.

Many do not see the connection between thoughts about the King and the service of the King; between the interior silence, which seems to consist in immobility, and the continual detachment, which is the essence of supreme activity.

If we look closer, it will be seen that there is a strong, close, unbreakable link between the two. Find a recollected person, and he will be detached; seek one who is detached, and he will be recollected. To have found the one is to have discovered the other. The truth of this may be estimated by the ease with which the one or the other of these two types can be found.

Anyone who tries, on a given day, to practice either recollection or detachment cannot ignore the fact that he is doing a double stroke of work.

The habit of self-renunciation requires constant recollection

If the soul, to become fully Christlike, ought to live in entire dependence upon the Holy Spirit, and if it is not possible to live in complete dependence upon the Holy Spirit unless the whole life is recollected, it is evident that recollection, in the sense that has been explained, constitutes one of the most precious virtues that can be acquired.

Father Pergmayer, one of those writers who has spoken most emphatically on this subject, does not hesitate to affirm, "The shortest road to gain perfect love is to have God always present; sin is driven away, and the soul has no time to think of anything else or to complain and murmur. . . . The practice of the presence of God leads sooner or later to perfection."

Not to try to live in interior silence is equivalent to giving up the effort to lead a truly Christian life. The

Christian life is a life of faith, lived in the invisible for what is invisible. Anyone who is not in constant contact with the invisible world runs the risk of remaining always on the threshold of a true Christian life.

To quote the words of Father Gratry:

> We must give up living in the outer and more superficial enclosure of the soul; we should go within and penetrate into its deepest recesses. And when we have arrived at this point, we must still go further in, until we reach the center, which is no longer self, but God. There is the Master . . . and there it is that it may be vouchsafed us to abide with Him for a whole day. Now, once we have been permitted to pass a day with Him, we shall desire to follow Him everywhere like His Apostles, His disciples, and His servants. Yea, Lord, when I have the privilege of spending the entire day with Thee, I shall wish to follow Thee always.[20]

Solitude is the stronghold of the strong. Strength is an active virtue, and our power of keeping silence marks the level of our capacity for action. "Without this interior

[20] Auguste-Joseph-Alphonse Gratry, *Meditations*.

cell, we would be incapable of doing great things, either for ourselves or for others."

The weak and unstable dislike to be alone. The majority of people look to amusement to save them from exerting themselves. They lose themselves in what is nought so that self may not be lost in what is all. It was in the midst of the silence of the night that almighty God came to earth.

> Silence [writes Father Faber] has ever been, as it were, the luxury of great holiness. . . . So it is the first life which He, the eternally silent spoken Word of the Father, chooses for Himself. All His afterlife was colored by it. In His childhood, He let speech seem to come slowly to Him, as if He were acquiring it like others, so that under this disguise He might prolong His silence, delaying thus even his colloquies with Mary. Mary also herself, and Joseph, caught from Him, as by a heavenly contagion, a beautiful taciturnity. In His eighteen years of hidden life, silence still prevailed in the holy house of Nazareth. Words, infrequent and brief, trembled in the air, like music which was too sweet for one strain to efface another, while the first still vibrated in the listening ear.

> In the three years' ministry, which was given up to talking and teaching, He spoke as a silent man would speak, or like a God making revelations. Then, in His Passion, when He had to teach by His beautiful way of suffering, silence came back again, just as an old habit returns at death, and became once more a characteristic feature of His life.[21]

We think so much of appearances that we are unable to appreciate anything that does not appeal to the senses. Silence is the source whence springs effectual effort. The jet of water is forced silently to bore its way through the stone before it is able to burst forth bubbling into song.

It must be well understood that when silence is recommended, it is interior silence that is meant, which should be imposed upon the senses and imagination to avoid the liability of being taken out of ourselves in spite of ourselves at every moment. If the oven door is perpetually kept open, to adopt the simile used by St. Teresa,[22] the heat will escape. It takes a long while to raise the temperature, but a second is sufficient for it to run down. A crack

[21] Frederick William Faber, *Bethlehem*.

[22] St. Teresa of Avila (1515-1582), Spanish Carmelite nun and mystic.

in the wall will let in the icy outer air, and the whole process has to be begun again.

An excellent method of preserving interior silence is to keep exterior silence. This is the reason for the cloister and the grill. But even in the world, each one of us can make his own solitude, a boundary beyond which nothing can force its way unperceived.

It is not noise in itself that is the difficulty, but noise that is pointless; it is not every conversation, but useless conversations; not all kinds of occupation, but aimless occupations. In point of fact, everything that does not serve some good purpose is harmful. It is foolish, nay, more, it is a betrayal to devote to a useless objective powers that can be given to what is essential.

There are two ways of separating ourselves from almighty God, quite different from one other but both disastrous, although for different reasons: mortal sin and voluntary distractions — mortal sin, which objectively breaks off our union with God, and voluntary distractions, which subjectively interrupt or hinder our union from being as close as it ought to be. We should speak only when it is preferable not to keep silence. The Gospel does not say merely that we shall have to give an account of every evil word, but of every idle thought.

We must speed up our lives, as modern people express it, and get rid of everything that lessens the output; the spiritual life, more than anything else, requires this speeding up, for it is the most important.

The interest the majority of people take in things of no account — the noises in the street, the behavior of passersby, the flagrant empty-headedness of the daily papers, whether intentional or unintentional — is almost incredible. What a joy it would be if suddenly, by some unexpected good fortune, everything in the world that does not serve some good purpose were to come to an end; if those who have nothing to say were to keep silence, this life would be a paradise!

The cloister is what it is because there men and women learn how to keep silence. They do not always succeed, but at least they are learning, and that is a great thing. Elsewhere it is a lesson that is not even learned. Yet speech is a great art, and conversation a valuable pastime, perhaps the most precious in existence, but good use is not abuse. It is customary on the anniversary of the Armistice to keep a two minutes' silence: this silence is in memory of the victory of the Allied troops. If the world would learn how to keep silence, this practice of recollection would lead to many victories.

"If any man offend not in word, the same is a perfect man."[23] "And let every man be swift to hear, but slow to speak."[24]

Our usual habit is to behave in an exactly contrary manner. Everyone talks; no one listens, least of all to Him who most deserves to be heard: the interior Master. There are few perfect souls because there are few lovers of silence. Silence is the equal of perfection, not in all, but in a great many instances. Put it to the test — it is worth the trouble — and the result will be a revelation.

[23] James 3:2.

[24] James 1:19.

Part Two

The Practice of Prayer

Chapter Four

Learn how to pray well

A fiction that must be destroyed is that it is difficult to pray. Nothing is simpler, so long as we know how to set about it. No one wishes to deny the difficulties of prayer — difficulties for the most commonplace minds, as well as for more elevated souls. This modest little volume is not meant for the latter. It will suffice to send them to read the dramatic pages of St. John of the Cross;[25] there the laborious and successive stages whereby the soul is purified from earthly attachments are described by one who has the authority of a saint, and who has himself passed through each one of these stages, in which Mount Calvary is a close neighbor to Mount Tabor.

There remain, therefore, the difficulties experienced by ordinary people. They are due, in the majority of cases, to the lack of method in our mode of coming into contact

[25] St. John of the Cross (1542-1591), Spanish Carmelite mystic and reformer of the Carmelite Order.

with the supernatural world, to want of courage in exerting ourselves during prayer, or to failure to persevere in the presence of God in times of aridity, when sensible consolations are absent.

We must learn how to prepare for prayer, how to be active during prayer; and how to persevere in prayer. All the technique of prayer can be deduced from putting these three injunctions into practice.

Prepare for prayer

In the preceding pages, care has been taken to distinguish between two forms of recollection: the one due to the bounty of God, and the other, the result of our own efforts, coupled with the habitual grace of God.

It is clear that, in the first case, granted that God does everything, human activity will be reduced to the minimum. All that is requisite is that we shall hold in reserve some subject of converse with our Lord, in case He should cease from entertaining us Himself. It would be an interruption and a hindrance to try to interpolate our own reflections or queries when the Holy Spirit is making His communications to us. We are already in contact with God. What is the sense of behaving as if we had to use our own efforts to approach Him? Who would turn on the electric light when the sun is shining?

Let the soul remain tranquil and listen; that is the rule to be followed, although this does not imply inactivity.

Quite different is the type of recollection that is the outcome of our own exertions. God is close by, but hidden, as is His custom. He waits to reveal Himself until we shall ourselves pierce the veil that conceals Him.

To kneel down and then wait, without doing anything, would be often a clear loss of time. Heaven helps those who help themselves.

How can we help ourselves? In this manner: let us imagine that the mind is either full of distractions or quite empty. We have to introduce into its field of vision something that will induce it to think about these invisible realities. This will be either an abstract idea, a concrete fact, or some text. Then we apply our mind and will to it.

- *An idea.* Let us take the idea of death. I have a memory, an intelligence, and a will. I will bring these three faculties to bear upon this idea.

- *Memory* (which includes the imagination). I will try to recall all I know about death, its circumstances, and its sudden, unexpected appearance, and represent to myself a deathbed scene, as a whole and in detail.

- *Intelligence*. Man must die. Then I also shall have to die. Am I mortal or not? Yes, I am. Then I shall die, I who at this present moment am so full of life.

- *Will*. Since I must die, I ought to live with the thought of death ever before me and detach myself from all earthly things. Can I say that I am detached?

This is merely one example; a thousand others will suggest themselves, and in every case the method is the same.

This is not some ingenious artificial method; the mode of procedure, if procedure it may be termed, is one that is common to every reasonable human being when he reflects. He tries to remember some incident and weaves into one whole, by a process of induction or deduction, the data that his memory provides and, in consequence of them, decides as his reason orders him to do. St. Ignatius calls this method the Exercise of the Three Powers.

To complain of the technique of prayer is to forget that although the faculty of speech is quite a simple matter, to explain how the vowels and consonants should be pronounced is not so easy. The use of firearms is simple; the theory of warfare is complicated.

This form of prayer is called *meditation*. The word here is applied in its exact significance, for the term can be used in a wider sense, to include all the general methods of treating with God and as a synonym for *prayer*. We may say we are going to make our meditation, and not mean thereby the exclusive use of the exercise of the Three Powers, but any form of mental prayer.

One of these forms is called contemplation; here also the word is used in its restricted sense, for in its full significance, it implies the type of prayer adopted by lofty souls. Contemplation, as St. Ignatius understood it, is setting the mind to work, not upon an idea, but upon a fact.

Let us take the Annunciation. To avoid being overburdened at the outset, it is a good plan to divide the mystery into the beginning, the middle, and the end, or rather, before, during, and after. In each part we can take as the framework the persons, words and, actions. For instance, concerning the beginning (that is, before the appearance of the angel), we should consider:

- *Persons*. There is only one, Mary. I look at her, and first of all, I notice her general appearance, her attitude of recollection. Then I go into more details; I consider her features: her eyes, her hands, and so forth. This is not difficult. Next I look within at her thoughts, her affections. With the assistance of this easy method, who is there who is not capable of penetrating into the hidden meaning of the mystery?

- *Words*. There are none. I listen and drink in the silence. God does not make Himself known in the tumult. Have I not experienced this in my own case?

- *Actions*. There are none.

This can be continued for as long as is necessary. The second point is the coming of the angel Gabriel; here there will be words to be listened to; I take them one by one and weigh them. Thus I continue for each part of the meditation.

Let us give this method a fair trial and set to work conscientiously and not give it up after the first attempt. I will guarantee that if our converse with God is prepared beforehand and we have the courage to persevere, we shall find prayer no longer hard. There are difficulties in prayer, but they do not lie here. To contemplate only means to look at something or someone. We know what it means to use our eyes. So open them wide. The obscure world of faith is more luminous than we imagine; it is necessary only to wish to see.

I can make use of a concrete fact or an abstract idea as a means of approaching God in prayer. Or I can take a text, a psalm, a well-known prayer, whose meaning I wish to call to mind, or a verse of Thomas à Kempis's *Imitation of Christ*. Those who wish to penetrate deeply into the mystery of God within us can make use of a little book somewhat resembling the *Imitation* entitled *Vivre en Dieu*.

This manner of prayer is excellent for beginners and also for those who are tired; it is good for everybody, provided they cease using a book as soon as a thought or loving aspiration comes to them. Many persons who practice meditation come to prayer without having prepared for it: this, as we have said before, is a psychological error. It is more; it is an indelicacy. I am about to hold converse with *God*, with the Lord of all; it is important to emphasize this fact. Imagine that an important personage is coming to visit a city. Do you think that those whose business it is to receive him would say, "It is quite futile to make any preparations beforehand. We shall get through all right"?

Apply these words to the case we are considering; they are far more appropriate.

Be active during prayer

Even when we have prepared both ourselves and our subject for prayer, it must not be imagined that the simple fact of kneeling down will instantly reveal to us the treasures of the supernatural world. Pearls cannot be purchased for a few pennies. We must devise means, use our brains, and exert ourselves. The name pious *exercises* is very apt, and it was St. Ignatius, a keen observer, who called his book on Christian perfection the *Spiritual Exercises*.

In point of fact, very few persons really exert themselves — that is, force themselves to take pains during prayer. To "make our meditation" is, for many of us, to go over the exciting or soporific considerations of some writer in a more or less passive manner.

There are some good books of meditation in existence, but they are not numerous. Often the theme is overly elaborate and drawn out and written in a complicated and too literary style; sometimes it is too difficult and abstract, or is expressed in a wealth of theological terms that is unattractive and gives an air of being archaic and unreal.

Therefore, some persons will say: "If my meditation has to consist in dissertations of this kind, I prefer to give it up immediately. I shall never succeed."

Perhaps this reasoning is too severe; yet it must be recognized that certain manuals of meditation have, in part, at any rate, contributed to this false impression of mental prayer, and so spread the notion that it is something repellent, impractical, and far-fetched. Such an idea of prayer is far removed from the definition given by St. Teresa: "Prayer is a loving converse with God," or the answer made to St. John Vianney, the Curé, "I look at Him, and He looks at me."[26]

Our advice is that a book of meditations should not be used unless there is really no alternative. The reason for the difficulty is not that they are badly written, but because they contain someone else's thoughts and are not suited to our individual needs. There is nothing more personal than prayer.

You say that the sentiments suggested to you by this writer mean nothing to you. I can readily believe it; they

[26] St. John Vianney (1786-1859), patron saint of parish priests; known as the Curé d'Ars. Someone asked the Curé d'Ars for a definition of faith. The reply was: "It is speaking to God as if He were our fellowman."

are his own ideas and do not necessarily correspond with your mentality. Why, when you are meditating, should you use the thoughts and sentiments of someone else for the development of your subject? He may have good ideas. But they are not yours. Why not try to draw them out for yourself, as he has drawn them out for himself? His ideas may very probably have done good to him, but they have only a distant connection with you and the needs of your soul.

If, after having conscientiously tried to make use of your own powers, you can find nothing, then you cannot do better than call upon someone else's ideas. But, please, give yourself full credit first, and try to produce from your own store that which you are wishing to say to God.

The child who wants to speak to his mother does not first hasten to the library to look for a guide to conversation or a collection of polite speeches. No, he has his own little phrases, his smiles and caresses, and his mother is far more pleased with these prattlings than she would have been with the fine but unreal expressions in the book.

When we speak to God, it is not in the language of Bossuet, nor is that necessary. But if we put our heart into our prayers, our poor words will certainly find their way to God. And how much greater the profit to ourselves!

The subject matter of our meditations, apart from certain variations, is the mysteries of our Lord's life throughout the year taken in conjunction with the liturgical cycle of feasts. It is therefore a good plan to provide ourselves with a book of the Gospels as a foundation for prayer. Among many other books, there is one by Canon Weber, *Les Quatre Évangiles dans un seul*,[27] which gives the life of our Lord from the Gospels in one connected whole, without the repetition to be found from reading the Gospels separately; the different parts and the episodes in each are clearly divided.

With this slender volume as a basis, and by making use of one or another of the methods indicated earlier, it is very easy, after a little practice, to make our meditation. If it is an idea that is under consideration, the exercise of the Three Powers will be used; if a historical event, the contemplative method; if a text, a more or less searching or rapid working out of this or that saying of our Lord.

Here, it seems, is all that is required for the making of a good meditation, provided we are determined to take an active part in it and not to remain passive. There is no desire to be overly exclusive in suggesting the life of our Lord

[27] Le Chanoine A. Weber, *The Saint Évangile*.

as the subject for meditation throughout the year; it is the advice of the masters of the spiritual life. Some persons will like to take some word or thought from the Mass of the day, or a psalm, and so forth. Any subject is good that serves to nourish the soul; every method is of use if thereby good results are obtained.

It should be noted that activity in prayer does not mean to become an automaton, a mere piece of mechanism. That some persons, through excessive respect for method, will sooner go through the treadmill than allow the Holy Spirit free play in their souls is a proof, not that methods are of no use, but rather that there are clumsy people in the world. The value of a thing must not be judged by its abuse.

It is quite clear that, having carefully prepared the subject for prayer, which out of deference to the Divine Master we ought to do, if our Lord chooses to substitute another subject for the one we have selected, the rule is to adapt ourselves to the inspiration from on high, and not to cling to our own choice, whatever it may cost us to give it up. A subject that is self-chosen must always give place to one that it pleases the Master of the soul to suggest, and which, in His estimation, is preferable. We should always follow the leading of the Holy Spirit, and we should not venture to impose upon Him our own ideas.

Our activity in this case consists, not in awkwardly trying to insert our own phrases into the conversation, but in leaving free scope for the lesson that God is desirous of giving. Our efforts will be spent in repressing an ill-advised activity. We shall show our activity not so much by speech as in listening. There are chatterers in prayer as elsewhere; let us avoid it. If it pleases our Lord to instruct our soul in a more or less direct manner and without troubling about our preparations, let us not in any way hinder His action. All we have to do is to intensify our interior silence so as to give Him the opportunity of making quite clear all that he wishes to say. "You make the river bed," said our Lord to a Visitation nun, "and I will be the torrent."[28] To St. Margaret Mary[29] He said, "Place yourself in my presence as if you were a bare canvas." These words, *make* and *place yourself*, imply a form of passiveness that is singularly active.

To sum up: when the Holy Spirit leaves us to our own devices, we can make use of our own resources. When, on

[28] Mère Marie Ponnet of the Convent of the Visitation of Vaissieux.

[29] St. Margaret Mary Alacoque (1647-1690), Visitation nun who received revelations of and promoted devotion to the Sacred Heart of Jesus.

the other hand, He shows that He wishes to dispense with our own actions, then we ought to place ourselves humbly at His disposition and, as generously as possible, bend ourselves to His designs.

Persevere in prayer

Two important conditions for success in prayer may be said to have been fulfilled. We have made up our minds to prepare for prayer and to exert ourselves during prayer. It remains for us to persevere.

The soul is subject to the same weather variations as the body. The sun is not always shining brightly. Many dull days may be counted upon, without mentioning periodic returns of darkness. Let us distinguish between three types of prayer: consolation in prayer, desolation, and passive prayer. When God sends consolation, there is nothing easier than to persevere in prayer; therefore, it is unnecessary to waste time upon this point. But there are certain pitfalls that ought to be pointed out, which, although they would not lead us to abandon prayer, would lessen the value of it.

The first is to mistake sensible consolations for the true mystical touch of infused recollection, and to imagine that because we have experienced sensible sweetness in prayer, we have been favored with mystical graces. The advice given by St. John of the Cross is applicable to this case. After saying that the soul should "never separate itself from its loving attention to God," an injunction that does not touch upon this subject, he adds words which are strikingly applicable: "But never desire to obtain any extraordinary graces."

Does this mean that we ought not to long for the closest union with God? Certainly we ought to do so. But, to adopt the division made by the theologians, it is one thing to wish for an ever-increasing fullness of sanctifying grace, which is always highly desirable, and quite another, and most imprudent, to desire visions, revelations, and free gifts. St. John of the Cross evidently alludes to these last in his words.

In general, souls to whom these mystical favors have been vouchsafed are far from desiring them, above all at the outset. They are alarmed by them. An expert director, if he perceives solid piety and the signs of true mysticism, has to instill confidence in the soul. The union of these two elements is both less uncommon than certain rigorous minds will allow, and less frequent than other optimists imagine.

Another danger in sensible consolations is to think that because we are content, therefore God is pleased with us.

Yesterday we were struggling with besetting distractions, and we fought bravely against them. When we rose from prayer, there was not much enthusiasm left. Today we were in the seventh heaven; all went well from first to last and without much effort. God did everything. Now, it would be childish to conclude that the meditation of today is much superior to that of yesterday. In reality, the value of a meditation may be gauged by the intensity of charity shown at the moment, and it is quite possible that when we were struggling against distractions yesterday, there was more charity at work than today, when favors were received. In theory, merit is not measured by the amount of effort expended, but by the exercise of charity.

Father Lancicius states very clearly, "It is an impermissible scruple to accuse oneself of having made a bad meditation because we were unable to feel any pious affections." According to him, the following examples are deserving of censure:

"If idle thoughts before meditation are not repulsed [which presupposes that the meditation is made soon after rising]. If, during meditation, distractions are not driven away at the first warning of conscience. If meditation is not continued for the time allotted to it. If our attitude is not sufficiently respectful, so that we should be ashamed if suddenly surprised by some spiritually minded person if the eyes are allowed to look about at what is going on, or the ears to listen to what is being said." And he concludes with these words: "Apart from these instances, the meditation is always good" — words that will act as a stimulus to the zeal of some persons, and calm the anxieties of others.

In addition to these times of consolation, periods of desolation must be reckoned with. This is the stumbling block to the majority of fervent souls.

It is necessary to know the methods that God usually employs when He raises the soul to the way of perfection. At the commencement, He loads it with favors. This is in order to give it an idea of what He is, to free it from the bondage of the visible world, and to enable it to appreciate the invisible world. He is lavish with His favors, draws the soul to Him with many consolations, and sets it on fire with burning love and the longing to continue the converse that has been interrupted. The soul feels the attraction. And how should it not be glad to be in such sweet company? The words of St. Peter on the mount of the

Transfiguration rise spontaneously to our lips: "Master, it is good for us be here."[30]

Then suddenly everything changes. Sensible devotion in prayer, after having lasted for a long or short period, comes to an end — in some cases suddenly, in others more gradually. The brilliant sunshine is followed by a kind of night that is all the more dense because of the radiant sunlight that went before. The impression given is of someone passing from broad daylight into a tunnel or underground cellar.

Here it is that God is waiting. Some persons — and they are the larger number — lose heart, for they are less truly pious than they appeared to be, and were following God more for His favors than for Himself; therefore, now that prayer is no longer a delight, they abandon everything. They believe themselves to be generous, and perhaps others think they are; but in part, at any rate, they are unconsciously selfish. They were seeking not God, but themselves.

Now, it is God's wish that we should — if we may venture to use the expression — look not at His hands, but at His Heart, not at what He gives, but at what He is. This is

[30] Luke 9:33.

why on occasion He withdraws His sensible attractions and leaves us to the exercise of pure faith. He wishes to discover whether the soul is truly seeking Him or His benefits. God desires to dwell alone in the soul. He wishes to be loved for Himself, and so, sooner or later, He withdraws everything when He vouchsafes to raise the soul to higher stages of prayer, so that it may dwell with Him alone.

Hence these strange purifying experiences, both active and passive (the night of the soul and the night of the senses), through which God leads the soul. His aim is to reach down until there is nothing in the soul but Himself.

When pious writers refer to the solitude of God in the soul, they are alluding to this divine urgency. Happy are those whose generosity and ardor is strong enough to enable them to direct their lives toward this end, and who persevere unwearied in spite of periods of spiritual dryness and of desolation.

But we must clearly realize the line of demarcation that divides the truly interior soul from the pious dilettante who exerts himself only when it suits him. If, among the readers of these pages, there are any who at this moment are struggling in the dark night, beside our Lord in His Agony in the Garden of Gethsemani, let them understand that upon their perseverance depends the bestowal of graces, whose value they ignore, whence they will obtain a sanctified power of energy that will surpass their strongest hopes.

It remains to say a word about the prayer of quiet. To persevere in this apparently requires less effort than in the prayer of desolation. But in reality, it demands more energy. The reason for this lies in the fact that unless the spirit of faith is very strong in us, the supernatural life does not attract us, and to pray means to endeavor to come into contact with the invisible world.

To reach the invisible, or even merely to go in search of it, necessitates the breaking away from outward appearances and the pleasures of sense. When Moses went to find God on Mount Sinai, he left his sandals at the foot of the mountain and laboriously climbed up out of the plain. To climb alarms us; we like the flat ground and prefer to walk comfortably shod. How many persons are there who, if they were truthful with themselves, would have to cast away their sandals?

But let us consider the case of a really generous person. A difficulty of quite another order threatens to paralyze his loving transports. He longs to make acts of adoration, praise, and thanksgiving, but with what can he give praise or adore? He has nothing, for he is poverty itself. How can his feeble prayers ever attain to what is due to the infinite God? What has he that can be offered to God that is worth anything, and is not almost an insult? God is the great God, and he is only a creature. How dare he come into the presence of Him who is all in all? It is the struggle between Jacob and the angel.[31] The soul is vanquished at the outset; the angel is always victorious.

Too many people, when they pray, do not make use of their intelligence, or, if we prefer, we can say instead that they show by their prayers that they have not fully grasped what St. Paul calls the Christian mystery, the mystery of our incorporation with our Savior, Jesus Christ, in the unity of one Mystical Body: "I am the vine; you are the branches."[32] There is no difficulty for those who realize this great truth. If I had to love God and give Him praise by myself, or with my own powers, I would be quite incapable of it, and my acts of homage, before ever they left this plane, would be forced to acknowledge their powerlessness. But I am not asked to do this.

Only our Lord Jesus Christ is capable of offering to the Father the glory that is His due, and owing to a wonderful

[31] Gen. 32:24-28.

[32] John 15:5.

act of mercy, I am one with Jesus Christ. Not only has our Lord made Himself one with us in order to redeem us, but He has vouchsafed also to make each one of us a part of Himself. This is the meaning of these words: no longer have I to love with my own powers, for I have at my disposal, when I pray, the prayer of our Lord. Jesus does not wish to be complete without me; He has made me an integral part of Himself. My prayer is insignificant and beneath everything, but His prayer is mine; I am able to make use of it; nay, more, it is my duty to use it.

In Baptism I received the power of offering our Lord to His Father, not on behalf of all the faithful, for only the sacrament of Ordination confers this, but on my own account. In this consists the spiritual priesthood of which St. Peter speaks, an office so lofty that he, the first Pope, does not hesitate to call it "a kingly priesthood."[33] Some people do not like this title to be applied to the ordinary layman or laywoman, but there is no reason to be afraid of it; we should try to understand what it means. It is a grand word and expresses a great truth.

To pray as a Christian, to use this term in its strict sense, is to pray after the manner of the Church, who, every time

[33] 1 Pet. 2:9.

she prays, by virtue of our baptismal priesthood, makes oblation of Christ to His Father. There is too much self in the majority of our prayers — not that our goodwill can ever err in overgenerosity, or that the offering of our whole self is not always ardently desired by God, but in the sense that there is not enough of Jesus Christ in our offering.

We speak of Heaven and earth. But this is not correct. We have forgotten that there is a third factor. There is Heaven and earth, and, between the two, Jesus, the Mediator, with whom we are one. The right expression for our relations with God in prayer is to be found in the words of St Paul: "Your life is hidden with Christ in God."[34] Here are the three — God, Christ, and ourselves — with their relative value; we are nothing, yet it is for us to pour the drop of water into the chalice, which reminds us of our exact place as merely a drop of water; Christ, ever making mediation that rises to the Father for the glory of the Father and the redemption of the world; and above all God, the Holy Trinity, to whom be all glory and honor. It is the "through Him, with Him, and in Him," of the Mass. There is not enough of Jesus Christ in our prayer as "other Christs."

[34] Cf. Col. 3:3.

"Self must be forgotten completely," Father Guilloré advises; and these words, after what has been said already, are not in danger of being misinterpreted. "You should only look two ways, one way toward the divine operations of our Lord, which you have in your hands like a present, and the other toward the Father to whom it is being offered up. This is the meaning of 'putting on Christ.' "

"I can no longer keep my eyes on myself," writes one who fully understood the meaning of living in Christ. "I do not mean that I am no longer conscious of my miseries; on the contrary, it is only the experience of my frequent falls that has taught me fully to realize them. But what is that, what is this nothingness in comparison with the infinity of God? It seems to me that to stop there is to insult our Lord, who has paid the debt, and whose merits we have acquired. If I had not Christ with me, I would never venture to approach the Father, but with Christ as my support and clothed with Him, I dare everything, for I am rich with all His riches."[35]

[35] It must not be imagined that she made her union with our Lord an excuse for not combating her faults. We are a hundred leagues from this teaching of Luther and the *pecca fortiter et crede fortius*.

Chapter Five

Turn everything into prayer

We have seen that, to remain in a state of prayer, it is not necessary to be always actively praying.

Every action done for God rises to His throne as an act of homage. It constitutes a lifting up of our whole being to His supreme majesty, a recognition — which, although not always explicit, is nonetheless real — of His sovereign due, and is the filial act of the creature offering everything to his Creator and his Father.

In practice, what is required of one who wishes to pray always?

He must give to each of his intentions the maximum of supernatural perfection that is humanly possible. And in this he will be aided greatly if he tries to perform his actions with the maximum professional skill of which he is humanly capable.

In other words, he has to purify the underlying motives of all his actions, and he has to do his best under all circumstances.

Have a pure intention

We do not think sufficiently of the goodness of God in the mechanism of the doctrine of intention. When we reflect upon the pettiness of our habitual actions and the feeble result they produce, we are alarmed.

How do we spend the twenty-four hours of the day? In extraordinarily hackneyed actions. Eight hours or more in bed, one or two in feeding ourselves, and what about the rest of the time?

Even in the case of persons whose work is of a more exalted character — the artist, the writer, the poet — what is the value of their masterpieces in the sight of God, and how much of their time is spent in duties other than artistic labors and creative work? There are proofs to be corrected, publishing accounts to be reckoned, and other things. How is it possible to amass eternal merit with such trifles as the sweeping of a room for the mother of a family, or the cooking for a general servant, or the explanation fifteen times repeated of a passage from Caesar or Virgil for a classical master?

If a supernatural intention is introduced into the actions, large or small, of daily life, it is as if leaven had been added, for immediately they begin to have life and to rise heavenward. A hidden fermentation is working in them. They have been changed from insignificant detail into eloquent praise offerings to almighty God. That which was a lifeless atom is now a living poem.

Henceforward nothing is base or vile; the poet's verse, the sauce for the luncheon, the speculative theorizing at the Sorbonne University, or a bundle of posts standing in a corner of the carpenter's workshop — all these can be supernaturalized. And how is this miracle to be accomplished? By the intention.

We would indeed be unfortunate if God were to judge our acts on their own merit. It is only the privileged few who are permitted to do great things. We shall be judged by the motive of our actions; and what a consoling thought it is to know that an unimportant existence, inspired by high motives, is incomparably greater than that which the world calls a noble life, but which is paved only with petty motives.

The whole of man is in the will that lies behind the thoughts and affections, and not in the broom, the brush, or the pen. Happy is the life beyond the veil, where true values will be made plain; there it will be manifested to all men that those personages who performed startling deeds are nothing but gas bags, while the woman pointed out by

St. Francis of Assisi[36] to Brother Juniper, surpasses in supernatural dignity the lukewarm monk or nun.

It is not sufficient to admire the beauty of a good intention; we must realize the difficulties in the way. The greater number of our motives are "mixed." The case of the evildoer, who seeks to do wrong, may be laid aside. Here we are speaking of the good Christian, the fervent soul. There is no doubt that he is searching for God, but not God alone; it is God with the addition of some whim, some satisfaction of self-love, or the desire of well-being or of vanity.

The *Imitation* recommends that we have a "simple eye that aims at nothing but God"[37] — that is to say, an exclusively supernatural aim, which the multiplicity of human motives cannot alter or disturb. St. Ignatius proposes the same ideal to his sons: "That in all things, they may seek God, and God alone." We have here a counsel given by all the masters of the spiritual life, and one of which we should remind ourselves continually.

Man belittles everything with which he comes into contact. He is made of spirit and matter, and this dual

[36] St. Francis of Assisi (1182-1226), founder of the Franciscan Order.

[37] Thomas à Kempis, *Imitation of Christ,* Bk. 3, ch. 31.

characteristic makes itself visible in all that he touches. He is born of two parents and seems to have a mania for what is complex.

We should keep a watch over this habit and frequently examine the motives of our actions and purity of intention. The author of the book *Paraître* describes someone whose perpetual preoccupation was to "think of himself." What others are thinking, what they will say, or maybe what they might say — if we could only realize how little, as a general rule, others think about us, and still more how lacking in interest are their opinions, and how little they deserve to influence us!

The greater number of human beings are led by shadows. Let us cast a strong light upon them. For whom and for what object am I doing this? To win a smile of approval from Jack or Peter, for the probable approbation of Mrs. So-and-so, which often never comes off. Be done with it!

In certain cases, it is wise, before an action, to make a determined effort to get rid of this complexity, if it exists, so as gradually to succeed in suppressing it quite naturally on every occasion. But it is better still to get into the habit of acting from the highest motive that is apparent.

There is some work that I have to do. It can be done because it is my duty and the will of God; and this is a perfect motive. Or it can be done because it is a means of assuring my position and of enabling me to provide suitably for my family — also an excellent motive, but of a natural order and greatly inferior to the former, which was wholly supernatural. Or thirdly, it can be done because it makes people think well of me and gives me the opportunity of shining in the public eye, and this is a far less honorable motive. It must not be thought that all is lost because a lower motive may have intervened during the course of the action.

Clearly, if it is a case of a manifestly bad intention which entirely swallows up the former good intention so as completely to destroy it (we must note these two conditions) the result will be a bad action, and the gravity of this is to be ascertained according to the ordinary moral laws affecting sin.

But more often, the former intention remains. I give alms out of compassion and charity; the secondary intention that glides in is that others may see me, for example, but it does not totally destroy it, although it alters it a little by adding a purely human element to an act that at the first was entirely supernatural. The action remains good, but the merit is somewhat diminished by the intrusion of a less noble motive; the simplest method of getting over it is to address this upsetting underhanded intruder in the words of St. Bernard:[38] "I did not begin this for you, and I have no intention of finishing it for you."

Do your best in everything

The normal accompaniment of a perfect intention is the perfecting of our actions to do our best, as in the sight of God. If the complaints heard on all sides are to be believed, actions that are well done are becoming rare. A trade conscience is disappearing. Men do not work; they avoid it. There is no longer, as formerly, the same degree of solicitude to do "the best possible." Charles Péguy, in his book *L'Argen*, speaks thus on this subject:

> We have known this painstaking love of perfection to be shown both in the mass and in the smallest detail, and this pious craze for the "task well done" maintained and extended to its utmost limit. During my childhood at my home, I have seen the people recaning chairs as carefully and exactly as their forefathers used to cut building stones for the

[38] St. Bernard of Clairvaux (1090-1153), abbot and Doctor.

> cathedrals. . . . Take note that nowadays it does not really please the workmen to do nothing: they would prefer to work. They hear the call of their race, and their hands are aching to be busy. . . . But their clever leaders have explained to them that this is socialism, and that is revolution.

Can it be said of us Christians that the pagan influence of the world in which we live, the habit of taking things as they come, has not penetrated somewhat into our lives?

What kind of professional conscience has each one of us in our state of life? How do we fulfill our daily duties? Is the work that has to be carried through done as well as we are capable of doing it? If not, what can we expect? Because our Master is good and rewards the smallest act even when only half-finished, shall we be content to give Him only acts that are not complete, a portion of our labor and half the produce of our undertakings?

We often long that our lives might be different. We would like them to be full of other events and to have a varied career, that our home duties would be less monotonous and of a more startling character. It is no secret that no one is content with his lot. Everyone would like to change places with his neighbor.

Now, God does not ask us to do something different, but to do what has to be done *differently* — to change, not our daily actions, but the manner in which we perform them. To darn the linen or correct an exercise, if it is part of our duty, merits a heavenly reward.

Each one of us, if he carefully examines his conscience, will discover that on many occasions he slacks off or even goes on strike. The saints did not behave in this manner. Whatever had to be done they did, and here is the most elementary, as well as the most profound, mark of sanctity. Some of them accomplished great things, but they did not become saints for that reason, and they were permitted to do great deeds only as a reward for fidelity in small things. There are many among the blessed, such as St. John Berchmans,[39] who are honored precisely because, in a short life, they realized perfection in their ordinary actions.

One who was asked his opinion of Father Chevrier, the evangelist of Marseilles, replied, "I know nothing about him except that he always keeps his door shut." The answer was made half-jokingly, but it was expressive, for it

[39] St. John Berchmans (1599-1621), Jesuit who followed the "little way."

implied complete self-control and fidelity in small things. To live a life of uninterrupted prayer that will beautify the grey monotony of our daily duties — who is there who could not become a saint in this way?

The great secret of a fervent life is to take as our ideal the maxim: "Act on all occasions as our Lord would have acted, had He been in our place." And it is to be noted that this is not an imaginary situation, more or less fictitious, but a reality. Each one of us in a state of grace is a living member of Christ, and therefore the acts we perform from a supernatural motive, Christ, as head of the human race, accomplishes in us and by us.

How would Christ fulfill this humble detail of my life? I must do it in the same manner.

If we adopt this counsel as the practical guide for our lives, we shall not have to look elsewhere for the road to sanctity; it is found already, and there is no more rapid or efficacious method.

Chapter Six

Develop a spirit of prayer

To take trouble over our prayers and to make our whole existence into a life of prayer are the requisite conditions for a true and close union with God. To these two points must be added a third, which is to make as many aspirations to God as possible during the course of the day. We shall see how this practice is to be carried out and what are its advantages.

Frequently offer brief, spontaneous prayers to God

We are convinced that the majority of souls who crave for holiness would ask for nothing better than to think often of God. But how is this possible?

First, we can train ourselves to think of God from time to time. The easiest method, to begin with, is to make an act every time there occurs some marked change of occupation. "If we can," writes St. Teresa, "let us practice many times a day the exercise of the presence of God, or at least now and then. . . . The recollection of the Companion within us, were it to last only a moment, would be of an immense profit to us."

Fénelon enters into more details:

> Profit by the moments in the day when your mind is only partially occupied with external things to think of God interiorly; for example, do your needlework in the simple and familiar presence of God. It is only while we are talking that recollection is less easy; nevertheless we can often recall to our minds a general thought of God that will act as a check on our words and will repress the susceptibilities of self-love in our dealings with our fellow creatures.
>
> We should be careful not to take too large a share in all that is said and done, and not to let these things fill our minds. Once we have seen what God demands of us in each instance, that is sufficient, and we can stand apart from all that follows. In this way the center of the soul will remain free and tranquil. . . .
>
> An excellent method of keeping ourselves in this interior solitude and freedom of spirit is, at the

> finish of each act, to bring all our reflections to a full stop and to give up all afterthoughts, whether of joy or sorrow, for these are some of the greatest hindrances. Happy the mind that dwells only upon what is of importance and thinks about each act only when it is the right moment to do so.

Then, after some further excellent advice, he conclude with these words: "Let us separate ourselves from all pleasures that do not come from God, and restrain useless thoughts and daydreams and the repetition of idle words.

Another passage from his works deserves mention:

> A brief recollection of the presence of God during meals, especially when they last a long time and there are many pauses, will serve to keep you within the limits of sobriety and to fortify you against excessive daintiness. There are moments at table when conversation lags because the guests are busy assuaging their appetites; this is an opportunity to give a thought to God. But all this should be done only so long as the thought and the wish for it come naturally into the mind without being forced.[40]

[40] François Fénelon, *Instruction and Advice*, Vol. 1.

These last words of Fénelon, "without being forced," should be remembered. The great law that governs the spiritual life, taken as a whole, is to avoid carefully all that can hinder "the holy liberty of the children of God"[41] that is to say, everything that curbs it, and prevents its free spontaneous action, and disturbs the mind so that it loses its peace and serenity.

We have read in the lives of some of the Fathers of the desert and in the biographies of certain saintly persons of our time, how they reached the most alarming figures in the number of brief, spontaneous prayers they offered.[42] It is recorded of St. Leonard of Port Maurice,[43] for example,

[41] Cf. Rom. 8:21.

[42] In the well-known *Vitae Patrum*, it is related of a saintly recluse that he raised his heart to God a hundred and three times during one conversation; and it is noteworthy that the hermits and early monks were unused to making long prayers. St. Augustine, in a letter to Proba, writes, "It is said of our brothers in Egypt that they prayed frequently, but that their prayers were very short, like darts shot heavenward, and the reason for this is interesting: it was for fear that the attention would end in becoming dulled and be extinguished finally if the prayer were prolonged."

[43] St. Leonard of Port Maurice (1676-1751), Franciscan priest who promoted the Stations of the Cross devotion.

that he made the resolution to repeat the invocation "My Jesus, mercy," a thousand times a day, either mentally or vocally. It was revealed to St. Mary Magdalen of Pazzi[44] that St. Aloysius[45] made unceasing aspirations that, to use an archaic expression, were shot like arrows from a bow up to Heaven; and she herself made the offering of the Precious Blood fifty times a day for the souls in Purgatory. St. Francis Xavier[46] repeated so frequently the words "O Most Holy Trinity!" that the heathen learned the habit of saying it also, although they had no idea what it meant. Father William Doyle, the well-known Irish chaplain during World War I, wrote in his diary six months before his death, "I have a clear inspiration that God asks me to make a hundred thousand aspirations in a day. I feel that our Lord asks this in reparation for His priests."

To reach divine union, is it necessary to seek to emulate these privileged souls and to aspire to these heights,

[44] St. Mary Magdalen of Pazzi (1566-1607), Carmelite nun who patiently bore grievous trials of body and spirit.

[45] St. Aloysius Gonzaga (1568-1591), Jesuit who ministered to plague victims.

[46] St. Francis Xavier (1506-1552), Jesuit missionary to the East Indies.

or at least to force ourselves to make these stupefying mathematical calculations? Not at all.

If it is good in principle that our brief prayers should be as numerous as possible, and that the interval between them should be as short as can be, it is also important that the rhythm of their frequency should be subject to the following two rules laid down by spiritual writers, Alvarez de Paz in particular, because he always tries to establish the exact equilibrium between the exertions prompted by generosity and the need of the soul for rest. The first is to guard against the weariness that speedily leads to distaste, and the second is to follow the leading of grace, for the Holy Spirit does not demand the same measure from all.

It may be noted that a certain type of distaste comes not from overexertion, but from pure laziness, and therefore is not a lawful motive for abandoning our good practices. But as soon as our conscience, aided, if necessary, by the advice of our director, tells us before God that we ought to bring our good practices to an end, then it is our duty to do so. The habit of monthly recollection and the annual retreat, above all, have in part the object of adjusting these difficulties in our spiritual life.

Whatever happens, we should never be surprised, and, above all, on no account be discouraged, if, in spite of our good resolutions — and it is only these circumstances to which we are referring — we do not at the outset attain to the allotted number of prayers, or if we discover that they are fewer today than yesterday. Man is well known to be an inconstant being, and while on this earth, he is much less likely to march on from one victory to another than to be perpetually retracing his steps.

Father Caussade, in his book *Abandonment to Divine Providence*, dwells upon this fact: "No one should be surprised that a day when recollection is easy is followed by another crowded with distractions, for such is our condition in this present life. These variations are necessary, even in spiritual matters, so as to keep us in a state of humiliation and of dependence upon God. The saints themselves went through these alternations."[47]

All this is very edifying, some persons will say, but our difficulty lies neither in the initial generous impulse nor in the wise manner of putting it into practice. We ask for nothing better than to think about God. But how can we remember to think about Him? When we are carried away by feelings that get the upper hand and dominate us, how

[47] Jean-Pierre de Caussade, *Abandonment to Divine Providence*, Vol. 2, letter 17.

can we manage to free ourselves at certain moments and pierce through to the supernatural, even if only in a lightning flash?

We have seen how the practice of daily meditation (praying carefully) and the exercise of the virtue of continual detachment (turning everything into prayer) — that is, an elevation to God by a pure intention and not a descent to self by following some whim of the moment — will facilitate our contacts with the invisible world. But it may happen, even after a carefully prepared meditation and a scrupulous effort at detachment, that a person is so engrossed by external affairs and a victim of circumstances that he will find great difficulty in recollecting the explicit presence of God. He may pass several hours, a complete morning, or the whole day without a single thought of his Divine Guest or without making one brief, spontaneous prayer. He wanted to remember Him, but he forgot to do so. What can be done?

As the world of sense is the great obstacle, the best method is to try to connect a pious thought with some ordinary act, thus turning an enemy into an ally; to utilize some detail of our everyday life to remind us of the spiritual world. St. Ignatius, as an experienced psychologist, is careful to base his scheme of particular examen upon this characteristic of human nature, for he advises us to combine the spiritual considerations with an exterior attitude or gesture.

For example, we determine that every time we pass some sacred figure, or a crucifix, or even when performing some commonplace action such as leaving the house or going into a room, or similar acts, they will remind us of the presence of God. Peasants used to make a knot in their handkerchiefs so that they might not forget some detail. Father Maunoir, after his missions in Brittany, asked his congregation to sew a heart-shaped piece of stuff on their sleeves, red for the men, and blue for the women, so that, in the middle of their work in the fields or in the home, the sight of this colored patch might call to their minds the thought of God. The repetition of the *Angelus* serves the same pious purpose.[48]

[48] The *Angelus*, traditionally prayed three times a day — in the morning, at noon, and in the evening — recalls the Incarnation: *The angel of the Lord declared unto Mary, and she conceived of the Holy Spirit. Hail Mary . . . "Behold the handmaid of the Lord. Be it done unto me according to thy word." Hail Mary . . . And the Word was made flesh and dwelt among us. Hail Mary . . . Let us pray. Pour forth, we beseech Thee, O Lord, Thy grace into our hearts, that we, to whom the Incarnation of*

Is there any danger that this frequent withdrawal into the interior life may be detrimental to the duties of our state of life? Not at all, if common sense is used. On the contrary, as St. Francis de Sales[49] is careful to remark, it cannot fail to put more heart into our work and to make us more conscientious and generous-minded in our work. "Note clearly," he writes, "that the practice of aspirations is neither difficult nor incompatible with your occupations, and far from diverting or lessening your attention to your business, it will render it easier and more efficacious."

It is evident, all the same, that the more manual the type of work, the less risk there is of its being in any way interfered with by the explicit exercise of the presence of God. The more intellectual the occupation we are engaged upon, the more it absorbs all our thoughts, and only by making a violent effort is it possible from time to time to break off and interpose a thought or say a word about God. In such a case, we would be misunderstanding our duties if we were to attempt such a thing. If this type of

Christ, Thy Son, was made known by the message of an angel, may, by His Passion and Cross, be brought to the glory of His Resurrection. Through the same Christ our Lord. Amen.

[49] St. Francis de Sales (1567-1622), Bishop of Geneva.

prayer hinders our work, then it must be sacrificed, so that the work may be properly done; before all things come the duties of our state, as has been said already.

St. Ignatius of Loyola, when he was a university student at Paris, felt himself suddenly overpowered by the realization of God's presence during the lectures. Acts of divine love came bursting forth from his heart and followed one another without interruption. He seemed to be in Heaven. That is true, but he was not attending to the class. He quickly realized that his studies were bound to suffer from these holy transports, so he asked God to repress them in order that he might be able conscientiously to complete his studies. Here is an intelligent form of piety.

But which are the best aspirations? Are there some that should be preferred to others?

The answer to this question is that each person should choose what he prefers; this is the main point. At one time, his inclinations will lead him to follow some inspiration from his prayers, or from the words of the Liturgy, or perhaps it may be rather the cry of the soul who is in the purgative way: "My Jesus, mercy; have pity on me!" On another occasion, the aspirations will turn toward the illuminative way: "Jesus, be to me a Jesus!" which was the favorite invocation of St. Philip Neri,[50] or the popular prayer "Sacred Heart of Jesus, I have confidence in Thee!" Other persons may choose aspirations suggested by the unitive way, which are the best of all and which more readily minister to its needs, such as, "O Blessed Trinity!" the exclamation of St. Ignatius, or "My God and my all!" of St. Francis of Assisi and many others.[51]

Without denying the utility of these suggestions, it may be added that a person who has no special learnings or attractions might use the Sign of the Cross or the Glory Be as aspirations of the highest value. It is good in general that our spiritual life should have its own fund to draw upon and not be encumbered by foreign vegetation. Before adopting pious practices and methods, let us first utilize what we have already tried. How man times in the day do we make the Sign of the Cross and say the Glory Be, especially if we have an office to say. The Glory Be was the favorite aspiration of St. Jerome. He sent it to Pope Damasus, who decided to add it to the breviary at the end of each psalm. It is impossible for the priest to think of the

[50] St. Philip Neri (1515-1595), founder of the Congregation of the Oratory.

[51] See also Alphonsus Rodriguez, *Christian Perfection*, Vol. 1, ch. 3.

words in each verse as he repeats his office, but what an easy and helpful way it is to try to recollect himself, or rather, to recollect the Holy Trinity in each Glory Be! What better reminder of the presence of God!

At this point, it will be useful to draw attention to the enormous advantage gained by those persons who have chosen, not the presence of God in all around us, but His presence *in* us, as the center of their spiritual life.

The search for God present outside demands a certain effort of the imagination, which results in a greater struggle and subsequent fatigue. The return to God present within us presupposes a simple glance of faith. The divine indwelling in a soul in a state of grace is a reality that requires no composition of place, nor that, in order to reach it, I should set off on a sort of audacious and fantastic pilgrimage to the confines of space. I have only to enter into my interior, and God is there.

Father Brou remarks, "Of all the methods of trying to enter into the presence of God, this one [to find God within the soul] is perhaps the most efficacious — at least for those who have the habit of prayer — and is the one which the saints most recommend."[52]

[52] Alexander Brou, *St. Ignatius, Master of Prayer*.

The words "In the name of the Father" do not cause me to think of a Father millions of miles away, or a Father who dominates me with His immensity so that my heart is more frightened than softened, but of a Father close by and within me — a Father who is there, and, to use an expression of Father Faber, who finds my soul the *home* of His Son, who is waiting for me at the door of my heart, and of the Holy Spirit, who intervenes in the conduct of my life so as to impart to it its eternal merit, who does everything with me and will not leave me for one instant alone.

We have seen how the thought of God present in our souls through grace is the great dogmatic truth on which a life of recollection can be most easily founded.

Everyone who has become familiar with this thought has an admirable method of practicing union with God, whether alone or in company, and of utilizing his surroundings as a means of leading him back to his center.

When we are alone with ourselves, a double self accompanies us always. If we have sufficiently developed the spirit of faith; if we realize the gift of God and truly believe; if, for us, the words "God is within us" are not only a beautiful phrase, a fine theme for a pious dissertation, but an undeniable fact that exists; if the expression

"We are the living tabernacles of Christ and in very truth His holy temples" has the value of reality for us — then can it be impracticable or difficult to be recollected on all occasions?

When we go into a cathedral or a church, instinctively we lower our voice, and we walk quietly. The great God is present, the Divine Host: let us be silent and adore.

Whatever we have to do, whether it be our business, some household shopping, recreation, or a course of study, so long as it is our duty, it will be quite impossible to get away from Him who is living and dwelling within us.

We are a living cathedral. Each one of us is his own chapel. And provided we are in an state of grace, God lives and dwells within us. What then?

The conclusion to be drawn is very simple and easily reached. It is that we must live and act as if we were dwelling in a church in the presence of the tabernacle.

The Holy Eucharist is not the only sacrament of the Real Presence; there are two, Baptism and the Holy Eucharist. The presence of the three Persons of the Holy Trinity in us through Baptism is no less real than the presence of our Lord in the tabernacle; the difference lies in the mode of Their presence, not in the reality. How comes it, then, that when we leave the church, we behave as if the Real Presence has ceased? It is because we have not sufficient faith and that, in practice, we do not know the gift of God.

Our spirit of recollection outside the church should be as profound as it is within the church. The monk, a disciple of St. Bernard, who composed the *Meditationes pïissimae*, wrote, "Wherever thou art, be recollected. There is no need for a special place. Thou art thyself this special place. Art thou in bed? Then thy bed is itself a temple."

The sole difference will be due to the duties of our position here and there.

I go into church to join in some service or to say some private prayers. But when I go out, I carry with me my tabernacle, I bear within me the Real Presence. Therefore, all I have to do will be done in the company of the Divine Guest, with the *dulcis hospes animae*. I shall not become immobile in static adoration, because my duties oblige me to work. But I shall not work in a turmoil, without an aspiration of adoring love, for my faith reminds me of the Guest whom I bear within me, reminds me that I am a living ciborium.

I am busy because it is my duty. But I do not work without God, because the most high God never leaves me alone.

Can we imagine a more luminous doctrine, at any rate in principle, or one simpler or more stimulating and apt to incite the soul to make unceasing cries of appeal, a loving gesture, a sign that will testify to Him who is always present that we are not absent, but fully recognize the incomparable value of His continual presence.

"Faith tells us," writes St. Paul of the Cross,[53] "that our heart is a large sanctuary, because it is the temple of God, the dwelling place of the Holy Trinity. Often visit this sanctuary; see that the lamps are lit — that is to say, faith, hope, and charity. Frequently stir up your faith when you are studying, working, or eating, when you go to bed and when you rise, and make aspirations to God."

In a seventeenth-century book, entitled *Practices for Keeping in the Presence of God*, we are recommended to give "a simple but loving thought to God present within us." By *simple* is implied that it can be done without pictures, acts, or mental reasoning and effort of the brain. Nor does this manner of thinking of God get into the way of occupations. It assists them; it is easier to work in the presence of a friend. By *loving* is meant that this exercise is

[53] St. Paul of the Cross (1694-1775), founder of the Passionist Order, who had gifts of prophecy and healing.

always accompanied by a secret longing to please God as a sign of our love for Him present in us, but it is not necessary to make a particular act of the love of God.

St. Teresa is the great authority on this matter. It is to her we should listen, and we need not hesitate to give a long quotation from that fine chapter 30 of the *Way of Perfection*.

> St. Augustine tells us that after searching for a long time to find God in the things that surrounded him, he discovered Him at last within himself. Meditate deeply on these words, for it is of great profit for anyone who has difficulty in recollecting himself to understand this truth: to know that it is not necessary for him to raise himself to Heaven in order to converse with his divine Father and find his happiness with Him, nor to elevate his voice so as to be heard; God is so near that He hears the slightest whisper from our lips and the most secret thought. We have no need of wings to go in search of Him. Let us enter into the solitude and look within us; it is there that He is. Let us talk with Him in great humility, but also with love, like children talking with their father, confidently telling

> Him our troubles and begging Him to help us, and recognizing above all that we are not worthy to bear the name of His children.

Then, in order to reassure those persons who will be astonished to see her pushing her practices to such far-reaching consequences, she adds these words: "Those who are able to recollect themselves in the manner that I have just described should know that they are walking on an excellent road, and they will not delay in drinking of the fountain of life."

There follows an injunction to underestimate no longer the gift of God, as is so often done: "If men were careful to remind themselves that they possess a Guest of such majesty, it would become impossible for them to devote themselves with such blind enthusiasm to the things of this world, for they would see how worthless they are beside those that they possess."

She ends with this following valuable advice:

> For myself, I own that I never knew what it was to pray with satisfaction until He Himself vouchsafed to teach me this salutary method. Let him who desires to acquire this habit of the presence of God never weary of working little by little to gain mastery over

himself, by recalling his senses within himself. Far from losing, he will find therein a great gain for his soul, that of retrenching the exterior use of the senses and of making them subservient to his interior recollection. If he speaks, let him try to remember to address the One in the depth of his heart. If he listens, let him not forget that he must listen interiorly to Him who speaks within. In short, let him consider that if he will, he can always enjoy this divine company.

Let him practice this many times a day, if possible; if not, let him at least practice it sometimes. Provided that, in the end, he becomes accustomed to it, he will sooner or later derive great benefit from it. When once this divine Master has given him this grace, he would not exchange it for all the treasures of the world. In the name of God, since nothing can be gained without labor, do not grudge the time and application that you have given to it. I assure you that, with the help of our Lord, you will succeed in one year, or perhaps six months.

A last word remains to be said on this important matter. Even in the world, in our customary and necessary contact with others, our household duties, our works of charity and of apostolic zeal, our society and business relations, the full realization of the gift of God will be of greater assistance than anything else in keeping the recollection of the presence of God.

God is living in us. But He lives also in the neighbors who move around us. Here also He is living or wishes to live; therefore, knowing that we are surrounded by tabernacles, either actual or by destiny, what an easy reminder they become of the three divine Persons.

Nor is there here any effort of the imagination, or laborious composition of place, which some persons declare to be beyond them. It is sufficient to consider that which is a reality. There is no need to construct, simply to make a statement; not to create, only to realize the value of this truth.

Let us imagine the case of a young mother busy with the multiple cares of her children. She must not say, "Union with God is impossible for me." She is surrounded with tabernacles of the Real Presence. Her little ones are baptized? Yes! Then God is living in them.

This master, this factory hand, this foreman, this worker, this schoolchild, our colleagues, and those we employ — are they not, if not in fact, at any rate potentially and by destiny, the bearers of Christ? Why look for anything else in them? Or at least why should we not see in them a1so, and above all, this one dominant fact? The "gift of God" is not meant only for us. It is also for them. They were created and placed in the world for a divine destiny. Our Lord shed His Precious Blood for them. Their earthly work is nothing else but their means of reaching Heaven and of enjoying by grace the anticipated possession of the three Persons of the Holy Trinity, while awaiting the fullness of glory.

A deeper understanding of this doctrine will undoubtedly help us to remember these facts.

Reap the benefits of aspirations

It is natural that aspirations and the exercise of the presence of God should be recommended by the teachings and personal experiences of the great spiritual writers and saints. One or two extracts of a specially striking character are added to those that have been given already.

St. Ignatius of Loyola writes:

> We should look for the presence of God in all things, in our conversations, our walks, when we are using

our eyes, listening, or thinking, when we are eating, and in all that we do. This manner of meditating, which causes us to find God in everything, is easier than the method that obliges us to exert ourselves, to elevate the mind to the consideration of more abstract truths. This salutary practice, if we dispose ourselves rightly, will be rewarded by a gracious visit from our Lord, even if it lasts only for the duration of a short prayer. Let us accustom ourselves to offer our troubles and difficulties frequently to God, and remind ourselves that we accept them out of love for Him, sacrificing our own wishes to be of service in some way to His divine majesty, by aiding those for whom He accepted death that they might live. We should examine ourselves upon these two points.[54]

"The shortest road to attain to divine charity," says Louis of Granada, "is to raise our hearts to God by our strong affections and by desires that are on fire for His love by conversing with Him with respectful confidence, and keeping ourselves always recollected in His presence."[55]

[54] St. Ignatius of Loyola, *Epistles*.

[55] Louis of Granada, *The Love of God*, ch. 9.

St. Francis de Sales and St. Leonard of Port Maurice give the same advice.

St. Francis de Sales writes, "The essence of real devotion lies in this exercise of spiritual retreat [recollection] and in aspirations. It can supply the lack of other prayers, but if it is missing, nothing can take its place. Without it, it is impossible to follow the contemplative life properly, and the active life will be a failure." He continues speaking of this "retreat of the heart," with the words: "It is here, Philothea, that I wish you to be most docile in following my advice, for it is upon this that your spiritual progress is most dependent."[56] And during the retreat preparatory to his consecration, the great Bishop made this resolution: "I will do my best to make aspirations during the day."

The celebrated Italian missionary St. Leonard of Port Maurice echoes the same idea: "Would you like to have your paradise anticipated upon earth? And the company of someone who will lead you rapidly to perfection? . . . Live in interior recollection, and walk in the presence of God." Then, speaking of himself, he says, "My vocation is mission work and solitude. My mission is to be always

[56] St. Francis de Sales, *Introduction to the Devout Life*, ch. 13.

working for God. All the rest is nothing." And each one of us has a like vocation, if only we would realize it.

The saints and spiritual writers are so unanimous and impressive in their recommendations that there must be wonderful advantages to be gained by the habit of aspirations and the practice of the presence of God. And this is quite true.

The first of these advantages is that prayer and detachment become easier, and as we have seen, they are the two fundamental methods of attaining to union with God.

To render prayer less difficult, we are told: "It is quite certain that when we love something, the thought of it comes often into our minds, but it is true, also, that this frequent thinking about it will greatly increase our love. One who is faithful in recollecting the presence of God frequently will soon be all on fire with love, and in proportion as his love increases, so his thoughts of Him will become so continuous that he will not forget Him anymore."[57]

Not only does prayer like this become easier by the exercise of the presence of God, but also throughout the day the life of interior silence, so necessary for union with God, will be facilitated A solitude in which we perceive

[57] D'Argentan, *Le Ciel dans l'âme chrétienne*.

only the emptiness of life is not very attractive; but if we have the skill to people it with thoughts of the supernatural, then this solitude appears to be no longer dark and sad, but rich and splendidly dowered, and overflowing with life, and how alluring! Only those who cultivate the presence of God, and the habit of frequently raising their hearts to Him, can know, as Cardinal Manning expressed it, "that solitude and silence are full of reality."

In the same way, the use of aspirations facilitates detachment. We are usually so craven-hearted because we do not realize clearly for whom and for what reason we ought to gain mastery over ourselves; the thought of God, particularly when it is inspired by ardent love, acts upon the dying embers of our life like a breath of wind, which blows away the dust that has accumulated and awakens the spark, kindling it into flame.

These words do not exhaust all the advantages of the use of the exercise of the presence of God and of aspirations. There is much more to be said. There is no better method of developing a state of continuous moral union with God than the frequent repetition of these acts of union.

The term *moral union* is used because, as was said at the beginning of these pages, a continuous actual union is impossible, save by a special grace of infused recollection, owing to our very limited powers of attention.

At the commencement, there should be a reasonable effort to think of God for a certain number of times and to offer Him our different actions. Then, little by little, will come an ever-increasing desire to do more.

There should be nothing feverish or hurried, but a harmonious, virile, and loving development of the spirit of faith, so that, supernatural habits having become natural, we turn back to the center of all, dwelling within us, whenever nothing external demands our attention, to the service of the King. As soon as I am obliged no longer to work for God, I will think about Him; this is the rhythm of the practice of a recollection that aims at being both prudent and intense.

Thus, we shall possess, or are preparing ourselves to possess, a continuous union with God; the habit of raising ourselves to God has such a part of our lives that it may be called uninterrupted. It is not a case of saying words, but the heart remains clinging to God, the will is one with the will of God, and the volatile mind, which is so often distracted and not always through its own fault, is so attentive to purify or offer its intentions before, during, and after the occupations of each moment of the day, that, in truth, to borrow the comparison of St. Francis de Sales, the soul resembles a child who is picking flowers by the roadside, but never lets go of his father's hand. St. Thomas calls this a habit, a stable quality that assists us to act without difficulty. It is characteristic of a habit that it is something that comes easily, and the habit of prayer, in common with every other habit, is the fruit of perseverance.

A modern philosopher gives a good description of the gradual self-mastery that is always progressing until at last the habit of union with God becomes quite easy:

> The first step in interior progress consists in the development of certain psychological states. At first, the mental powers are turned in upon themselves, and having but rarely the opportunity of outward expression, they seem to acquire an importance they do not possess as yet. . . . The faithful Christian, whose love for God at first consists in a brief recollection night and morning, reaches the point of being able to perceive the continuous presence of the object of his love with him, even when a voluntary effort seems to be required to enable him to fix his attention upon vocal prayer; he feels himself from henceforward to be obsessed by the need of

praying. . . . Soon he begins to look upon the universe as merely a transparent veil, behind which the presence of the Creator can be everywhere discovered. . . . Every creature, however humble, is an image of the face of God. Thus, he recognizes in all the mark of God, revealing their common origin, so that, in his eyes, they will appear as all brothers and sisters of each other and of him. In this way, out of his first effort to turn himself toward God, has grown up, like the tree from an acorn, a devouring love of God and of all things in God.[58]

Then we have the lyrical language of Father Gratry:

There are persons who feel more than others the need of rest and of the return to the center of life. When such a one has united himself to God, has tasted of His fullness, after having been subject to the insufferable vanity of the outer life, there comes a time when all business, all external work, all going into the world becomes impossible to him. The world is then like an intruder who comes to

[58] Etienne Gilson, "*Essai sur la Vie Intérieure*," *Revue Philosophique*, January/February 1920.

> disturb a feast, and the necessity of submitting to it draws tears; as when some tedious business comes upon us in the midst of an inspired work, or some stranger, one we know by sight, but whom our heart knows not, comes in and takes up the best part of the day that had been promised to prayer and study, and by his words, countless and unprofitable as the dust, distracts our attention, which fails at every word to concentrate itself. Even thus does the outward life weary these persons and increase their longings for the eternal rest. It is true that such a ripeness for death is rare among men but the least can comprehend and accept it.[59]

If we are among these "least," we ought not to be too surprised that we have still to struggle to attain to the desired habit of recollection, and we should have confidence.

But how comes it that, in spite of a normal power of attaining good habits and the assistance of grace that trebles our own powers, we do not reach our goal?

St. Teresa avows, "For years I was going through the trial of being unable to fix my thoughts. . . . It was extremely

[59] Gratry, *Meditations*.

painful. But I knew that our Lord condescends to keep us company when we go to Him humbly to ask Him for it. If a year passes without our getting there, very well then! Let it be several years. I assure you that we can reach it, and we can with effort acquire the habit of living thus in the company of the greatest of all Masters."[60]

On his side, Louis of Granada says:

> The holy King David tells us that he lived always in the presence of God, when he uses the words: "I set the Lord always in my sight."[61] Do the same thing, and raise your heart continually to God, without violently forcing yourself, but letting your mind lose itself in loving simplicity in this sovereign Divinity. Do not be distressed to find your thoughts so often distracted, owing to human weakness: try quickly to recollect yourself and offer yourself to God anew. If you have the courage to go through this combat without being shaken for some length of time, I venture to assure you that the custom will become second nature, and that not only you will

[60] St. Teresa of Avila, *Way of Perfection*, ch. 26.

[61] Ps. 15:8 (RSV = Ps. 16:8).

> no longer have any difficulty in recollection, but even that you will never give it up. You will be like the fish that cannot live out of water, and if it finds itself outside, does all that it can to return.[62]

The person who easily and habitually turns toward God in the midst of his ordinary occupations, possesses a moral union that is continuous.

If, at this moment, it should please God to call us to a state, not of acquired recollection, but to that which is infused, nothing will have done more to prepare us for this favor — as far as it is possible for us to prepare for what is a pure gift of God — than the effort to remain in the presence of God as continually as possible, through the exercise of the spirit of faith and of loving generosity.

St. Teresa, whose advice upon this point is based on her own personal experiences, declares, "In this way, you are laying down a solid foundation. And if it please our Lord to raise you to higher things, He will find you ready."[63] St. Teresa was here referring principally to the habit of recollecting the presence of God within us.

[62] Louis of Granada, *Amour de Dieu*, ch. 9.

[63] *Way of Perfection*, ch. 29.

This is not the place to seek to penetrate into the realm of "higher things," to which the saint alludes. To do so would be to go beyond the scope of this book, which is to show how, with the aid of grace such as is common to us all, *and the cooperation of our own personal resources*, it is possible to reach union with God and to arrive at that degree of recollection which is obtainable through our own spontaneous efforts.

For those others to whom God vouchsafes the gift of infused recollection, whether by a touch or a prolonged state, they no longer require counsels and rules, but should practice the virtues of docility and humility and make the donation of their whole selves without reserve.

The Holy Spirit Himself takes over their guidance, and He leads them without the sound of words.

The writer of this volume may also be silent, and utilize the silence as it ought to be used at the termination of a work, in asking our Lord to bless those who will read these pages and to give to them the largest possible share in the joys of "praying always."

Conclusion

If this little book were to have only one reader, and that reader unknown to us but so greatly beloved in Christ Jesus, we would not wish to end it otherwise than with these words of advice.

They come from the lips of a master of the spiritual life, perhaps the greatest of all masters, St. John of the Cross: "Why have you been putting off for such a long time your going to God, since *at this very instant* you can occupy your heart with loving Him?"

If, on the other hand, he is one who has already resolved to belong to God, and his whole heart is occupied at this moment with loving Him, but he would like to love Him more, a passage from the same *Spiritual Sentences* of the saint will go far in reassuring him: "If you desire a clear and simple view of God in your soul, and that He should there shed His radiancy, do not busy yourself among creatures; on the contrary, empty yourself of them; then you will walk in the midst of the divine light."

Raoul Plus, S.J.

(1882-1958)

Raoul Plus was born in Boulogne-sur-Mer, France, where he attended the Jesuit college. In 1899 he entered the Jesuit novitiate in Amiens and was ordained there. Because of laws that persecuted religious orders at that time, Fr. Plus had to leave France in 1901 and did not return from this exile for ten years, during which time he studied literature, philosophy, and theology in Belgium and Holland. He also taught courses in the field of humanities.

At the advent of World War I, Fr. Plus enlisted as a soldier, and subsequently as chaplain, and later was awarded the *Croix de Guerre* and the *Medaille Militaire* for his heroism. It was during this time that he began to write, producing his first two books, which were followed by a host of works on various aspects of the spiritual life, and in particular, about the presence of Christ in the soul.

After the war, Fr. Plus taught religion at the Catholic Institute of Arts and Sciences in Lille and became a well-loved spiritual director for the students. During school vacations, he gave retreats for priests and seminarians and wrote several books concerning priests.

In his lifetime, Fr. Plus wrote more than forty books aimed at helping Catholics understand God's loving relationship with the soul. His words consistently stress the vital role of prayer in the spiritual life and seek to show how to live out important spiritual truths. His direct, practical style renders his works invaluable for those seeking to know Christ better and to develop a closer union with Him in their souls.

Sophia Institute Press®

Sophia Institute

Sophia Institute is a nonprofit institution that seeks to nurture the spiritual, moral, and cultural life of souls and to spread the Gospel of Christ in conformity with the authentic teachings of the Roman Catholic Church.

Sophia Institute Press fulfills this mission by offering translations, reprints, and new publications that afford readers a rich source of the enduring wisdom of mankind.

Sophia Institute also operates two popular online Catholic resources: CrisisMagazine.com and CatholicExchange.com.

Crisis Magazine provides insightful cultural analysis that arms readers with the arguments necessary for navigating the ideological and theological minefields of the day. *Catholic Exchange* provides world news from a Catholic perspective as well as daily devotionals and articles that will help you to grow in holiness and live a life consistent with the teachings of the Church.

In 2013, Sophia Institute launched Sophia Institute for Teachers to renew and rebuild Catholic culture through service to Catholic education. With the goal of nurturing the spiritual, moral, and cultural life of souls, and an abiding respect for the role and work of teachers, we strive to provide materials and programs that are at once enlightening to the mind and ennobling to the heart; faithful and complete, as well as useful and practical.

Sophia Institute gratefully recognizes the Solidarity Association for preserving and encouraging the growth of our apostolate over the course of many years. Without their generous and timely support, this book would not be in your hands.

www.SophiaInstitute.com
www.CatholicExchange.com
www.CrisisMagazine.com
www.SophiaInstituteforTeachers.org